My First Book about Planets

THE SOLAR SYSTEM
INCLUDES THE SUN AND 8 PLANETS (INCLUDING THE EARTH, WHERE WE LIVE!)

The Solar System

MARS

The planets circle around the Sun, and this is called orbits.

The Sun

The Sun is a star – a massive ball of hot gas that gives off heat and light. It's the only star in our Solar System.

We have 8 planets in our Solar System. These are in order from the Sun: MERCURY, VENUS, EARTH, MARS, JUPITER, SATURN, URANUS AND NEPTUNE.

There are also dwarf planets such as Pluto, moons and millions of asteroids, comets and meteoroids.

Our Solar System is in the Milky Way Galaxy

1. Mercury

MERCURY IS THE CLOSEST PLANET TO THE SUN

Mercury is the smallest planet in our Solar System (it's only a little bit bigger that Earth's moon).

It doesn't really have an atmosphere. It has extreme temperature changes and many craters.

A year on Mercury lasts 88 Earth days

Mercury is a terrestrial planet.

It has a solid rocky surface.

2.
Venus

IS EVERYONE SO HOT OUT THERE?

VENUS IS THE HOTTEST PLANET IN OUR SOLAR SYSTEM

Venus has a thick atmosphere, which traps heat, and is permanently covered in clouds.

It has many volcanoes and it is about the same size as Earth.

It spins the opposite direction of Earth and most other planets.

A year on Venus lasts 225 Earth days

Venus is a terrestrial planet too.

3. Earth

EARTH IS THE ONLY PLANET ON WHICH WE KNOW THERE ARE PLANTS AND ANIMALS LIVING

Earth is made of rock and is the only planet where water is liquid.
It is a terrestrial planet too.

It takes 365 days for the Earth to travel around the Sun.
We call this a year.

Earth has one moon

The Moon

The moon is a ball of rock that orbits around our planet.

NOT EVERYTHING IN THE SOLAR SYSTEM ORBITS AROUND THE SUN.

MOONS ORBIT AROUND PLANETS.

Our moon is the only place in the Solar System that man has travelled to.

It is much smaller than the Earth.

It has many craters.

4. Mars

MARS IS SOMETIMES CALLED THE RED PLANET BECAUSE THE ROCKS THAT IS MADE FROM ARE RED

It is the closest planet to Earth, and is slightly smaller than Earth.

It has a thin atmosphere, and its average temperature is $-63°C$.

It has two moons. Their names are Phobos and Deimos.

A year on Mars lasts 687 Earth days

5.
Jupiter
JUPITER IS THE BIGGEST PLANET IN OUR SOLAR SYSTEM

JUPITER IS THE BIGGEST PLANET IN OUR SOLAR SYSTEM

Jupiter is made of gas and is one of the four 'gas giants'.

Jupiter has rings, but it's hard to see them.

A year on Jupiter lasts 11.8 Earth years

Jupiter has 80 moons.

One of them, Ganymede, is bigger than Mercury.

6. Saturn

SATURN IS FAMOUS FOR HAVING RINGS OF SMALL PIECES OF ICE AND DUST AROUND IT

Its rings were first observed in 1,610 by Galileo Galilei.

It is the second largest planet in the Solar System, and it is a 'gas giant' like Jupiter.

A year on Saturn lasts 29 Earth years

Saturn has 63 moons.

7. Uranus

Uranus is the coldest planet in our solar system

URANUS IS THE COLDEST PLANET. IT HAS AN AVERAGE TEMPERATURE OF -220°C

It is an ice giant and it looks blue due to the methane in its atmosphere.

It also has faint rings.

Like Venus, Uranus rotates in the opposite direction as most other planets. And also, it rotates on its side.

A year on Uranus lasts 84 Earth years

Uranus has 27 moons.

8. Neptune

NEPTUNE IS THE FARTHEST PLANET FROM THE SUN.
IT IS 30 TIMES AS FAR FROM THE SUN AS EARTH.

Neptune is also an ice giant and it also looks blue due to the methane.

It also has rings, but it's hard to see them.

A year on Neptune lasts 165 Earth years

Neptune has 14 moons.

Dwarf Planets

These are other objects in our Solar System that are much smaller than the other planets. Their names are Ceres, Pluto, Haumea, Makemake and Eris.

Asteroids, Comets and Meteoroids

Asteroids are small rocky bodies that orbit the Sun

Comets also orbit the Sun, but they are made of ice and dust

Meteoroids are small pieces of asteroids or comets. Sometimes they enter our atmosphere and start to vaporize. They are then called meteors.

If they don't vaporize completely and land on Earth, they are called meteorites.

Thank you, thank you, thank you
for your purchase!

If you are happy with
My First Book about Planets,
please help me writing a positive review
on Amazon!